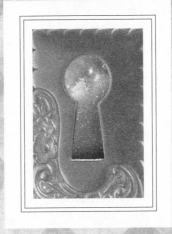

This journal belongs to

DATE BEGUN

DATE ENDED

A *Life God*

REWARDS

JOURNAL

Based on *A Life God Rewards*™
by Bruce Wilkinson

\text{WITH } DAVID KOPP

Multnomah®Publishers *Sisters, Oregon*

A LIFE GOD REWARDS JOURNAL
published by Multnomah Publishers, Inc.
© 2002 by Exponential, Inc.
International Standard Book Number: 1-59052-010-6
Cover image by Koechel Peterson & Associates
Scripture is from *The Holy Bible*, New King James Version.
Copyright © 1982 by Thomas Nelson, Inc. Used by permission.
Other Scripture quotations:
The Holy Bible, New International Version (NIV)
© 1973, 1984 by International Bible Society,
used by permission of Zondervan Publishing House

Multnomah is a trademark of Multnomah Publishers, Inc.,
and is registered in the U.S. Patent and Trademark Office.
The colophon is a trademark of Multnomah Publishers, Inc.
Printed in the United States of America

For information:
MULTNOMAH PUBLISHERS, INC.
POST OFFICE BOX 1720
SISTERS, OREGON 97759

02 03 04 05 06 07 08—10 9 8 7 6 5 4 3 2 1

᠕᠎᠍᠌᠋᠊

WHAT COULD TODAY MEAN
IN YOUR FOREVER?

Dear friend,

So few steps we take in our lives really change how we think, how we
live, what we expect...

Receiving Jesus' good news about eternal rewards was one of those
steps for me. One day I decided to believe that I was God's workmanship—
not just saved *from* my sin, but created in Christ Jesus *for* good works
(Ephesians 2:10). I began to see the extraordinary business of eternity hid-
ing in the ordinary business of everydayness. And my life changed *a lot!*

If you've read *A Life God Rewards,* I imagine you're in the middle of the
same kind of transformation. The thirty-one-day *A Life God Rewards
Devotional* and this accompanying journal have been created especially with
you in mind. Together, they will help you see and do the lasting good works
God has created you to do, starting today.

Use the pages of this spiritual journal to write down prayers, ques-
tions, and newfound Scriptures and to record God's amazing work in your
life. There's no better way to get the most out of life—or please Him
more—than to make every day and every act count for eternity.

May you meet your giving God anew each day in these pages. And may
you walk forward in faith and gratitude to live for Him!

Warmly,

Bruce Wilkinson

Now if anyone builds on this foundation with gold, silver, precious stones, wood, hay, straw, each one's work will become clear; for the Day will declare it, because it will be revealed by fire; and the fire will test each one's work, of what sort it is. If anyone's work which he has built on it endures, he will receive a reward. If anyone's work is burned, he will suffer loss; but he himself will be saved,

yet so as through fire.

1 Corinthians 3:12–15

"Blessed are you when men hate you,
        And when they exclude you,
And revile you, and cast out your name as evil,
        For the Son of Man's sake.
Rejoice in that day and leap for joy!
        For indeed your reward is great in heaven,
For in like manner their fathers did to the prophets."

LUKE 6:22–23

"For the Son of Man will come in the
    glory of His Father with His angels,
and then He will reward each according to his works."

MATTHEW 16:27

*A*nd you know that, of all truths, this is the truest,
    that the good and godly shall obtain the good reward
inasmuch as they held goodness in high esteem;
    while, on the other hand,
the wicked shall receive meet punishment.

CLEMENT OF ALEXANDRIA

∞

Everyone who competes in the games goes into strict training.
They do it to get a crown that will not last;
but we do it to get a crown that will last forever.

1 CORINTHIANS 9:25, NIV

None can become fit for the future life,
who hath not practiced himself for it now.

AUGUSTINE

_____

_____

_____

_____

_____

_____

_____

_____

_____

_____

_____

_____

_____

_____

_____

_____

_____

*Jesus said to him, "If you want to be perfect,
go, sell what you have and give to the poor,
and you will have treasure in heaven;
and come, follow Me."*

MATTHEW 19:21

＂*If you, then, though you are evil,*
  know how to give good gifts to your children,
how much more will your Father in heaven
  give good gifts to those who ask him!＂

MATTHEW 7:11, NIV

God can be as generous as He wants with what
belongs to Him.
If we argue with His amazing goodness,
it may be because goodness is
lacking in our own hearts.

A LIFE GOD REWARDS

"And everyone who has left houses or brothers or sisters
      or father or mother or children or fields for my
sake will receive a hundred times as much
      and will inherit eternal life."

MATTHEW 19:29, NIV

The Scripture is full, from beginning to end,
of the proposals of reward.
And the greatest characters have acted on this expectation.

JOSIAH PRATT

∞

His lord said to him, 'Well done, good and faithful servant;
you were faithful over a few things,
I will make you ruler over many things.
Enter into the joy of your lord.'"

MATTHEW 25:21

Even if we persuade only a few,
we shall obtain very great rewards,
for, like good laborers, we shall receive
recompense from the Master.

JUSTIN MARTYR

*W*hat is tested at the bema, the judgment seat?
    Your works. What you did with your life
will endure like gold, silver, and precious stones in a fire.
    Or it will burn up like straw—not a trace will remain,
no matter how sensible, enjoyable, or even religious
    these activities might have seemed while you were alive.

A LIFE GOD REWARDS

_____

_____

_____

_____

_____

_____

_____

_____

_____

_____

_____

_____

_____

_____

_____

_____

_____

_____

_____

Whatever good thing you do for Him,
*   if done according to the Word,*
is laid up for you as treasure in chests and coffers,
*   to be brought out to be rewarded before both men*
and angels, to your eternal comfort.

JOHN BUNYAN

And whatever you do, do it heartily,
as to the Lord and not to men,
knowing that from the Lord you will receive the
reward of the inheritance;
for you serve the Lord Christ.

COLOSSIANS 3:23-2

And let us not grow weary while doing good,
    for in due season we shall reap
if we do not lose heart.
    Therefore, as we have opportunity,
let us do good to all, especially to those who
    are of the household of faith.

GALATIANS 6:9–10

⚛

_____

_____

_____

_____

_____

_____

_____

Do you see your God in a fresh light?

He is a God who notices and cares about your every attempt, no matter how small, to serve Him.

He sees your upturned face, knows your heart, and cares about your faithfulness.

A LIFE GOD REWARDS

_____

_____

_____

_____

_____

_____

_____

_____

God is not unjust; he will not forget your work
and the love you have shown him as you have helped
his people and continue to help them.

HEBREWS 6:10, NIV

❦

"Lay up for yourselves treasures in heaven,
      where neither moth nor rust destroys
and where thieves do not break in and steal.
      For where your treasure is,
there your heart will be also."

MATTHEW 6:20–21

_____

_____

_____

_____

_____

_____

_____

_____

_____

_____

_____

_____

_____

_____

_____

Then He also said to him who invited Him,
"When you give a dinner or a supper,
do not ask your friends, your brothers, your
relatives, nor rich neighbors, lest they also invite you
back, and you be repaid.
But when you give a feast,
invite the poor, the maimed, the lame, the blind.
And you will be blessed,
because they cannot repay you;
for you shall be repaid at the resurrection

of the just."

Luke 14:12–14

If we are Christ's, we are here to shine for Him:
by and by He will call us home to our reward.

DWIGHT L. MOODY

_____

_____

_____

_____

_____

_____

_____

_____

_____

_____

_____

_____

_____

_____

_____

_____

_____

_____

＊＊＊

_____

_____

_____

_____

_____

_____

_____

_____

_____

_____

_____

_____

_____

_____

_____

_____

_____

_____

_____

Nothing is clearer than that a reward
is promised to good works,
in order to support the weakness
of our flesh by some comfort;
but not to inflate our minds with vain glory.

JOHN CALVIN

Let them do good, that they be rich in good works,
ready to give, willing to share, storing up for
themselves a good foundation for the time to come,
that they may lay hold on eternal life.

*In this world it is not what we take
up but what we give up that makes us rich.*

HENRY WARD BEECHER

Then I heard a voice from heaven say,
   "Write: Blessed are the dead
who die in the Lord from now on."
   "Yes," says the Spirit, "they will rest from
their labor, for their deeds will follow them."

REVELATION 14:13, NIV

God will reward every one according to his works.
    But this is well consistent with his distributing
advantages and opportunities of improvement,
according to his own good pleasure.

JOHN WESLEY

_____

_____

_____

_____

_____

_____

_____

_____

_____

_____

_____

_____

_____

_____

_____

_____

_____

_____

_____

_____

_____

_____

_____

_____

_____

_____

_____

_____

_____

_____

_____

_____

"Anyone who breaks one of the least of these
         commandments and teaches others to do the same
will be called least in the kingdom of heaven,
         but whoever practices and teaches these commands
will be called great in the kingdom of heaven."

MATTHEW 5:19, NIV

We ask how much a man gives;
  Christ asks how much he keeps.

ANDREW MURRAY

Jesus told parables about stewards
for an important and specific reason:
He would soon be going away.

During His absence, the business of His kingdom
on earth would be delegated to His followers.

They would be commissioned to spend their
lives greatly increasing His kingdom.

In the future, He would return,
ask for an accounting, and reward His servants.

A LIFE GOD REWARDS

~~~

Therefore, my dear brothers, stand firm.
    Let nothing move you.
Always give yourselves fully to the work of the Lord,
    because you know that your
labor in the Lord is not in vain.

1 CORINTHIANS 15:58, NIV

Look to yourselves, that we do not lose those things we worked for, but that we may receive a full reward.

2 JOHN 1:8

_____

_____

_____

_____

_____

_____

_____

_____

_____

_____

_____

_____

_____

_____

_____

_____

_____

For we must all appear before the judgment seat of Christ,
that each one may receive the
things done in the body, according to what he has done,
whether good or bad.

2 CORINTHIANS 5:10

∞

_____

_____

_____

_____

Whatever things might look like right now,
    on a day in the future, He will open His book of
remembrance, and the truth about His generosity,
    faithfulness, and justice will be evident to all.
Not one act of service in His name
    will have gone unnoticed or unrewarded.

A LIFE GOD REWARDS

_____

_____

_____

_____

_____

_____

_____

_____

_____

_____

The man who plants and the man
who waters have one purpose,
and each will be rewarded according to his own labor.

1 CORINTHIANS 3:8, NIV

*Treasures in heaven are laid up
as treasures on earth are laid down.*

JOHN W. DRAPER

_____

_____

_____

_____

_____

_____

_____

_____

_____

_____

_____

_____

_____

_____

_____

_____

_____

_____

_____

_____

"*But love your enemies, do good, and lend,*
hoping for nothing in return;
and your reward will be great,
and you will be sons of the Most High.
For He is kind to the unthankful and evil."

*G*ood works will have their reward.

　　It is our duty to be aroused by so great a promise,
to take courage not to weary in well-doing,

　　and to receive God's great kindness with true
gratefulness.

JOHN CALVIN

Do all the good you can,
By all the means you can,
In all the ways you can,
In all the places you can,
At all the times you can
To all the people you can
As long as ever you can!

JOHN WESLEY

Blessed is the man who perseveres under trial,
because when he has stood the test,
he will receive the crown of life that God has
promised to those who love him.

JAMES 1:12, NIV

...knowing that whatever good anyone does,
he will receive the same from the Lord,
whether he is a slave or free.

EPHESIANS 6:8

"And behold, I am
coming quickly,
and My reward is with Me,
to give to every one according

to his work."

Revelation 22:12

When you serve God, you are using God's
        money to accomplish His wishes.
But when you serve money,
        you are using God's money
to accomplish your wishes.
And when you do that, you will inevitably follow your
        human instincts to keep your money here.

A LIFE GOD REWARDS

_____

_____

_____

_____

_____

_____

_____

_____

_____

_____

_____

_____

_____

_____

"Sell what you have and give alms;
provide yourselves money bags which do not grow old,
a treasure in the heavens that does not fail,
where no thief approaches nor moth destroys."

LUKE 12:33

The wicked man earns deceptive wages,
    but he who sows righteousness reaps a sure reward.

PROVERBS 11:18, NIV

*T*herefore judge nothing before the time,
     until the Lord comes, who will both bring
to light the hidden things of darkness
     and reveal the counsels of the hearts.
Then each one's praise will come from God.

I CORINTHIANS 4:5

*M*ake your one aim in life
        the doing of the will of Jesus
in every circumstance, however important
or trifling it may seem.

Ignatii Brianchaninov

"If anyone gives even a cup of cold water
   to one of these little ones because he is my disciple,
I tell you the truth, he will certainly not lose his reward."

_____

_____

_____

_____

_____

_____

_____

_____

_____

_____

_____

_____

_____

_____

_____

_____

"Be faithful until death,
and I will give you the crown of life."

_____

_____

_____

_____

_____

_____

_____

_____

_____

_____

_____

_____

_____

_____

_____

_____

_____

_____

_____

_____

*The rewards are such as should make us leap to think on,
and that we should remember with exceeding joy, and
never think that it is contrary to the Christian faith
to rejoice and be glad for them.*

JOHN BUNYAN

The greatness of a man's power
   is the measure of his surrender.

WILLIAM BOOTH

*Now hope does not disappoint,
    because the love of God has been poured out in our
hearts by the Holy Spirit who was given to us.*

ROMANS 5:5

_One day in heaven will pay you, yea, overpay your blood,
bonds, sorrow, and sufferings;
it would trouble an angel's understanding to lay
the account of that surplus of glory
which eternity can and will give you._

SAMUEL RUTHERFORD

∽∞∽

The created world is but a small parenthesis in eternity.

SIR THOMAS BROWNE

*N*ow when Christ says: make to yourselves friends,
        lay up for yourselves treasures, and the like,
you see what he means: do good, and it will follow of itself
        without your seeking, that you will have friends,
find treasures in heaven, and receive a reward.

MARTIN LUTHER

*He who often thinks of God,
        will have a larger mind than the man
who simply plods around this narrow globe.*

CHARLES SPURGEON

The greatest thing a man can do for his heavenly Father
is to be kind to some of His other children.

HENRY DRUMMOND

_____

_____

_____

_____

_____

_____

_____

_____

_____

_____

_____

_____

_____

_____

_____

_____

_____

Therefore, we should seek from none other than the
*   Lord God whatever it is that we hope to do well,*
or hope to obtain as reward for our good works.

AUGUSTINE

If people would but provide for eternity
  with the same solicitude and real care
as they do for this life,
  they could not fail of heaven.

JOHN TILLOTSON

_____

_____

_____

_____

_____

_____

_____

_____

_____

_____

_____

_____

_____

_____

_____

_____

_____

_____

There are degrees of reward that are given in heaven.
I'm surprised that this answer surprises so many people
I think there's a reason Christians are shocked
when I say there are various levels of heaven
as well as graduations of severity of punishment in hell.

R. C. SPROU

For I know the thoughts that

I think toward you,

says the LORD,

thoughts of peace

and not of evil,

to give you a future

and a hope.

JEREMIAH 29:11